W9-BLZ-295

Warships

KATIE MARSICO

Children's Press®
An Imprint of Scholastic Inc.

Content Consultant

Matthew Lammi, PhD
Assistant Professor
Department of Science, Technology,
Engineering, and Mathematics Education
North Carolina State University
Raleigh, North Carolina

Library of Congress Cataloging-in-Publication Data

Marsico, Katie, 1980– author.
 Warships / by Katie Marsico.
   pages cm. — (A true book)
 Summary: "Learn all about warships, from how they have influenced history to how the
technology behind them has improved over time." — Provided by publisher.
 ISBN 978-0-531-22484-7 (library binding : alk. paper) — ISBN 978-0-531-22274-4 (pbk. : alk. paper)
 1. Warships—History—Juvenile literature. 2. Naval history—Juvenile literature. I. Title. II. Series:
True book.
 V750.M38 2016
 623.82—dc23   2015027428

No part of this publication may be reproduced in whole or in part, or stored in a retrieval system,
or transmitted in any form or by any means, electronic, mechanical, photocopying, recording, or
otherwise, without written permission of the publisher. For information regarding permission,
write to Scholastic Inc., Attention: Permissions Department, 557 Broadway, New York, NY 10012.

© 2016 Scholastic Inc.

All rights reserved. Published in 2016 by Children's Press, an imprint of Scholastic Inc.
Printed in China 62
SCHOLASTIC, CHILDREN'S PRESS, A TRUE BOOK™, and associated logos are trademarks and/or
registered trademarks of Scholastic Inc.
1 2 3 4 5 6 7 8 9 10 R 25 24 23 22 21 20 19 18 17 16

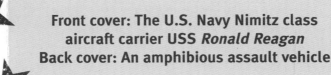

**Front cover: The U.S. Navy Nimitz class
aircraft carrier USS *Ronald Reagan*
Back cover: An amphibious assault vehicle**

Find the Truth!

Everything you are about to read is true *except* for one of the sentences on this page.

Which one is **TRUE**?

T or F   Teams of oarsmen powered the earliest warships.

T or F   The *Bismarck* was easily destroyed in battle.

Find the answers in this book.

Contents

THE **BIG** TRUTH!

Big-Time Battles!

The Spanish Armada was defeated in 1588.

The USS Independence has been in service since 2010.

Old Ironsides is on

CHAPTER 1

Ships That Have Shaped History

In August 1812, a wooden warship nicknamed Old Ironsides became an unforgettable part of U.S. history. At the time, the United States was battling Great Britain in the War of 1812 (1812–1815). It had been only 36 years since colonial leaders had declared independence from British rule. The United States was still a young nation, and Great Britain had one of the most powerful navies in the world.

More than 500,000 people tour Old Ironsides every year.

Beating the Odds

Nevertheless, Old Ironsides—formally named the USS *Constitution*—helped the United States demonstrate that it was a worthy opponent. On August 19, 1812, U.S. forces aboard the warship opened fire on Britain's HMS *Guerriere*. The *Guerriere*'s cannons returned fire. Despite being made from wood, Old Ironsides withstood the cannonballs, and the Americans were victorious. As a result, the ship earned both its famous nickname and a memorable place in U.S. history.

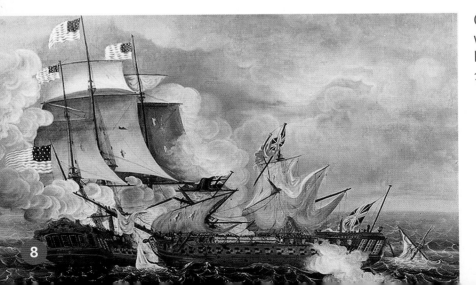

Old Ironsides was first launched in 1797.

Modern warships, such as this one in China, are used by countries around the world for defense and combat.

Critical to Combat and Defense

The story of Old Ironsides is just one example of how warships have played an important role in history. These **vessels** have traveled through war-torn waters since ancient times. But warships have not merely shaped the sea battles of the past. They also remain critical to defense and combat operations around the globe today.

South Korean warships patrol coastal waters for enemy submarines in 2010.

Warships are large boats used for military purposes. They often carry troops, weapons, **ammunition**, and aircraft. They are typically swift and sturdy. In many cases, warships must withstand enemy attacks in the heat of battle. In other situations, they patrol the water to help maintain peace and security.

Warships have influenced the outcomes of countless naval battles, or military battles that take place at sea. It's likely that warships will continue to have a similar impact on future conflicts. As a result, designers and engineers all over the world constantly work to create faster, stronger vessels. Their work is the latest step in a history that stretches back thousands of years.

Designing and building a warship is a long, complicated process.

Oarsmen rowed from belowdecks in a typical galley.

CHAPTER 2

Centuries at Sea

The earliest warships were galleys. A galley is a long, slender boat that relies on a crew of oarsmen to glide it across the water. Early galleys were usually used to ram into enemy ships to try to sink them. Sometimes, soldiers from a galley would climb aboard the vessel they had just rammed. Then they would fight hand-to-hand.

Warships were first used in ancient Rome, Greece, and the Middle East.

The Coming of Catapults

Starting in the fourth century BCE, however, navies began equipping their warships with catapults. These wooden machines made it easier to attack enemy ships without having to ram them. They used swinging arms to launch large stones into the air toward other vessels. The stones would put holes in ships and cause them to sink.

Catapults were used both on land and at sea.

Guns and cannons made warships more effective in battle.

Heavy Weapons

Warships were gradually improved over time. One huge leap forward came during the 14th century CE, when Europeans started mounting guns on their vessels. By the late 15th century, they were doing the same with cannons. However, the heavy cannons weighed down ships. This made it very difficult for the crew to row quickly. An increasing number of warships were fitted with sails to help power them.

Iron became a more common building material in the 1800s as many more factories began making it.

Industrial Advances

Warship technology went through even bigger changes during the 19th century. The invention of the steam engine provided an even more effective way to power huge, heavy ships. Around the same time, iron and steel also became more readily available as building supplies. These strong materials replaced much of the wood on warships. This made them better at repelling attacks from cannons and guns.

The *Dreadnought*

In 1906, Great Britain kicked off a new era of warships with the HMS *Dreadnought*. This legendary vessel was a major improvement over earlier ships. Despite its huge size, a powerful steam engine made it one of the fastest ships in the world at the time. Instead of being armed with a mixture of small and large guns, it was equipped with only heavy weapons. In the years ahead, other navies around the world attempted to build ships that could match the *Dreadnought's* speed and power.

World War II

By the time World War II (1939–1945) began, warships were improving rapidly. They were faster and larger than ever, and they were equipped with a wide range of weapons. Scientists had also developed radar technology. Ships used radar systems to send out radio waves that determined the location and speed of other moving objects. This allowed naval forces to launch more precise attacks on enemy planes and ships.

With the invention of radar technology, the crews of warships no longer had to rely on their eyes alone to spot approaching enemies.

An airplane prepares to take off from the deck of a British aircraft carrier during World War II.

World War II also saw the increasing importance of warships called submarines and aircraft carriers. A submarine can travel deep underwater. An aircraft carrier can transport airplanes. The planes take off from and land on its deck. This meant naval ships were no longer limited by the distance their guns could strike from. A carrier's planes could fly farther out.

Nimitz-class aircraft carriers are the largest warships in use by the U.S. Navy.

CHAPTER 3

Modern Military Vessels

Today, naval forces generally rely on seven main types of warships. These are aircraft carriers, cruisers, destroyers, frigates, corvettes, submarines, and amphibious assault ships. At present, aircraft carriers are among the largest warships in the world. Some are more than 1,000 feet (305 meters) long. That's about the height of New York City's Empire State Building!

 Aircraft carriers remain in service for decades.

Modern fighter planes need plenty of space to speed up as they take off.

Today's Aircraft Carriers

An aircraft carrier's length is part of what makes it so useful. These vessels need room for an onboard flight deck where planes can take off and land. The largest carriers are capable of transporting more than 80 combat aircraft at a time. Despite their size, the fastest aircraft carriers move at speeds of more than 35 miles per hour (56 kilometers per hour).

An Overview of Support Vessels

Cruisers, destroyers, frigates, and corvettes are classified as support vessels. These ships are typically smaller and speedier than aircraft carriers. They often travel with a larger **fleet** of ships to help protect them from attacks. Many support vessels are also capable of conducting independent strikes against enemy forces.

Large and small warships often travel together to assist one another as needed.

Cruisers are generally the largest of the support vessels. They are best known for carrying guided-missile systems. A guided missile is an explosive weapon that, after being launched, is directed toward a specific target by technology such as radar. Cruisers are used to fire guided missiles at targets on land as well as in the air and water.

A U.S. Navy cruiser launches a guided missile during the Iraq War.

A Swedish corvette patrols the country's coast.

Like cruisers, destroyers transport guided missiles. They are often used for patrols and search-and-rescue missions. They can also attack submarines, aircraft, and other surface warships. Frigates and corvettes are smaller than destroyers, but they perform a similar range of tasks. They typically don't have the missile-launching abilities of larger support vessels. However, they are effective in escorting **convoys** through the water.

Submarines can travel on the surface or dive deep underwater as needed.

Underwater Wonders

Unlike aircraft carriers and support vessels, submarines mainly operate below the water's surface. They're usually armed with guided missiles, **torpedoes**, and sometimes even **nuclear** weapons. Because these warships can remain hidden beneath the waves, they are used to conduct everything from attacks to **surveillance** and rescue missions. Some submarines can operate thousands of feet underwater.

From Sea to Sand

The word *amphibious* means "suited for both land and water." In amphibious attacks, militaries attack land targets from the water. Amphibious assault ships look a lot like aircraft carriers. However, their main purpose is to transport ground troops from water to shorelines. Like other modern warships, they became famous during World War II but are still in use today.

Amphibious assault ships carry smaller vehicles that troops can use to reach the shore.

Big-Time Battles

Many historic battles simply would not have been the same without naval vessels. In some cases, the outcomes of such conflicts have shaped the course of history.

The Battle of Salamis

The Battle of Salamis took place in 480 BCE in straits along Greece's southeastern coast. Persian forces were trying to invade the Greek mainland. Their 1,207 massive warships dwarfed the Greeks' 371-vessel fleet. However, the Persians still lost. Their boats became jammed in the narrow straits. This allowed the Greeks to ram and board them.

The Battle of Lepanto

The Battle of Lepanto took place in October 1571 CE. Christian and Turkish galleys fought each other off the coast of southwestern Greece. Both fleets were roughly the same size, but the Christians' vessels won. The battle was one of the final naval conflicts to revolve around oar-driven galleys.

The Battle of Hampton Roads

On March 9, 1862, the CSS *Virginia* and the USS *Monitor* clashed. The battle took place in a harbor called Hampton Roads in southeastern Virginia. It became one of the most famous naval conflicts in the U.S. Civil War (1861–1865). It was the first time in history that fighting erupted between two ironclads. (An ironclad was a 19th-century warship protected by iron plating.) Though it wasn't clear which side won, the battle represented the new era of metal warships.

The Battle of Leyte Gulf

This World War II battle was one of the largest naval conflicts in history. It occurred in late October 1944 near the Philippine islands. The battle was mainly fought between Japanese forces and U.S. and Australian troops. It featured hundreds of warships, including submarines and both surface and amphibious vessels. The Japanese lost a total of four aircraft carriers, three battleships, 10 cruisers, and 11 destroyers. U.S. and Australian losses were limited to three aircraft carriers and three destroyers.

The Spanish Armada was notable for its incredible size.

World-Famous Warships

Like Old Ironsides, many warships have become famous for their roles in historic battles. Among the most famous ships in history were the vessels of the mighty Spanish Armada. Also known as the Invincible Armada, Spain's attack force featured about 130 vessels, 2,500 guns, 8,000 sailors, and nearly 20,000 soldiers when it set sail in 1588.

The Spanish Armada was commanded by Alonso Pérez de Guzmán, the Duke of Medina-Sidonia.

The Invincible Armada

Spanish emperor Philip II planned to use the Armada to invade Great Britain during the Anglo-Spanish War (1585–1604). The Armada's commanders were confident their massive fleet would succeed. However, they were soon proven wrong. Great Britain used long-range guns to severely cripple the Armada. Only half of Spain's fleet survived, and the invasion was repelled.

After about eight hours of combat, the surviving ships in the Spanish Armada retreated.

German leader Adolf Hitler salutes the *Bismarck* as it sets out on its first mission.

Beware the *Bismarck!*

Shortly after World War II began, Germany added a warship called the *Bismarck* to its naval fleet. It measured 823 feet (251 m) long. This made it one of the largest battleships any European power had ever constructed. In addition, it was fitted with a great deal of steel armor. To Great Britain and other nations that were fighting Germany, the *Bismarck* posed a major threat.

Despite its incredible size and power, the *Bismarck* was in service for less than a year before its destruction.

In late May 1941, the *Bismarck* destroyed one of Great Britain's top ships and seriously damaged another at the Battle of the Denmark Strait. In retaliation, British naval and air forces chased the German vessel throughout the Atlantic Ocean. Though the *Bismarck* was greatly outnumbered, taking it down was no easy task.

Between May 26 and May 27, the *Bismarck* was assaulted by British planes and a total of three British warships. It was hit more than 400 times. In addition, naval experts estimate that it was hit by as many as 12 torpedoes. Finally, a torpedo hit the *Bismarck*'s rudder. With no rudder, the crew couldn't steer the ship, and the British were able to sink it.

The *Bismarck* suffers a direct hit in its battle with British forces in late May 1941.

An Enduring Vessel

The USS *Midway* is recognized for being a long-lasting and **versatile** vessel. The U.S. Navy kept it in service from 1945 until 1992. During this period, the *Midway* cruised through every ocean in the world.

A Timeline of the USS *Midway*

1945–1955
The USS *Midway* is the largest ship in the world.

1975
Survivors of the Vietnam War flee to safety aboard the USS *Midway*.

The *Midway* was involved in combat during the Vietnam War (1954–1975) and the Gulf War (1990–1991). The ship was also used to deliver **humanitarian** aid to people living in war-torn countries. It provided similar relief to areas that had been affected by natural disaster. Today, the *Midway* is permanently docked in San Diego, California, where it serves as a museum.

1991

After a huge volcanic eruption, the USS *Midway* brings aid to the Philippines.

2004

The USS *Midway* Museum opens in San Diego, California.

Today's warships are much more maneuverable than those of the past.

CHAPTER 5

A Look Ahead

The need for warships will not go away anytime soon. Wars will continue to affect civilizations in the future just as they have throughout history. As militaries develop new weapons and strategies, the engineers who design and build warships must respond accordingly. As a result, the years ahead will likely see increasingly powerful naval vessels.

Littoral combat ships are designed to move quickly in areas near shorelines.

The USS *Gerald R. Ford* undergoes testing in a dock.

The Latest Plans

Precise plans for future warships aren't always shared with the public. For security reasons, such information is often kept a secret. Nevertheless, the few details that are available paint an impressive picture. For example, the U.S. Navy soon hopes to add an aircraft carrier named the USS *Gerald R. Ford* to its fleet.

At a cost of $13 billion, the warship will be an expensive addition. However, the *Gerald R. Ford* will be able to launch a greater number of planes each day than older aircraft carriers. In addition, the ship's crew will be capable of firing a wider range of weapons, including **electromagnetic** catapults called rail guns.

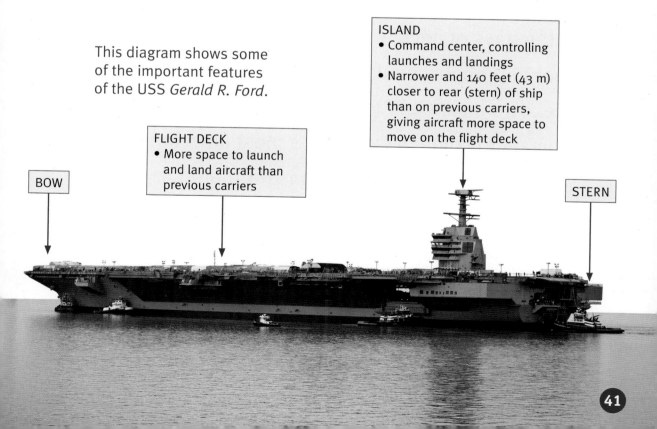

This diagram shows some of the important features of the USS *Gerald R. Ford*.

ISLAND
- Command center, controlling launches and landings
- Narrower and 140 feet (43 m) closer to rear (stern) of ship than on previous carriers, giving aircraft more space to move on the flight deck

FLIGHT DECK
- More space to launch and land aircraft than previous carriers

BOW

STERN

Like many older ships, the HMS *Victory* is kept on display for visitors to tour.

Forever Fantastic

In the days of ancient galleys and catapults, people probably couldn't imagine the sleek, speedy cruisers and guided missiles used today. In years to come, even today's most amazing warship technology will become outdated. It will be replaced by things that may even seem impossible today. But no matter how advanced tomorrow's technology becomes, the incredible warships of the present and past will forever remain engineering wonders.

Sunken Secrets

Planning for the future involves learning from the past. Sunken warships are a valuable source of information about historic battles and naval technology. In some areas, the mysterious wreckage of dozens of vessels litters the bottom of the sea. Divers frequently explore these sites to take pictures. They also retrieve equipment and artifacts. Their findings often provide missing pieces to stories that enhance our understanding of history. ★

Current maximum length of aircraft carriers:
1,092 ft. (333 m)

Number of warships Japan lost during the Battle of Leyte Gulf: 4 aircraft carriers, 3 battleships, 10 cruisers, and 11 destroyers

Number of warships the United States and Australia lost during the Battle of Leyte Gulf: 3 aircraft carriers and 3 destroyers

Number of warships in the Spanish Armada: About 130

Cost of the USS _Gerald R. Ford_: $13 billion

Did you find the truth?

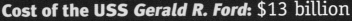

(T) Teams of oarsmen powered the earliest warships.

(F) The _Bismarck_ was easily destroyed in battle.

Resources

Books

Colson, Rob. *Warships*. New York: PowerKids Press, 2013.

Cooke, Tim, ed. *Warships*. Mankato, MN: Smart Apple Media, 2013.

Nagelhout, Ryan. *Aircraft Carriers*. New York: Gareth Stevens Publishing, 2015.

Visit this Scholastic Web site for more information on warships:
★ www.factsfornow.scholastic.com
Enter the keyword **Warships**

Important Words

ammunition (am-yuh-NISH-uhn) — things such as bullets or shells that can be fired from weapons

convoys (KAHN-voiz) — groups of vehicles or ships that travel together for convenience or safety

electromagnetic (i-lek-troh-mag-NET-ik) — relying on a magnet that is formed when electricity flows through a coil of wire

fleet (FLEET) — a number of ships, planes, or cars that form a group

humanitarian (hyoo-man-uh-TER-ee-uhn) — having to do with helping people and improving their lives

nuclear (NOO-klee-ur) — having to do with the energy created by splitting atoms

straits (STRAYTZ) — narrow strips of water that connect two larger bodies of water

surveillance (sur-VAY-luhnts) — the process of observing an area to gather information

torpedoes (tor-PEE-dohz) — underwater bombs shaped like a tube that explode when they hit a target

versatile (VUR-suh-tuhl) — able to function or to be used in many different ways

vessels (VES-uhlz) — ships or large boats

Index

Page numbers in **bold** indicate illustrations.

About the Author

Katie Marsico graduated from Northwestern University and worked as an editor in reference publishing before she began writing in 2006. Since that time, she has published more than 200 titles for children and young adults. Ms. Marsico hopes to one day visit the USS *Midway* in San Diego, California.

PHOTOGRAPHS ©: cover: Mass Communication Specialist 2nd Class Jacob Estes/U.S. Navy; back cover: Mass Communication Specialist 1st Class Vladimir Ramos/U.S. Navy; 3: WINDN/AP Images; 4: Time Life Pictures/Getty Images; 5 top: Newagen Archive/The Image Works; 5 bottom: Mass Communication Specialist 2nd Class Daniel M. Young/U.S. Navy; 6: John Gaffen/Alamy Images; 8: U.S. Navy; 9: Dai Zongfeng/ColorChinaPhoto/AP Images; 10: Kim Jae-hwan/AP Images; 11: Roger Bamber/Alamy Images; 12: WINDN/AP Images; 14: Lourens Smak/Alamy Images; 15: age fotostock/Alamy Images; 16: Everett Collection/Superstock, Inc.; 17: War Archive/Alamy Images; 18: Bettmann/Corbis Images; 19: AP Images; 20: Mass Communication Specialist 3rd Class Anthony N. Hilkowski/U.S. Navy; 22: Mass Communication Specialist Seaman Derek Poole/U.S. Navy; 23: Stocktrek Images/Getty Images; 24: Intelligence Specialist 1st Class Kenneth Moll/U.S. Navy; 25: epa european pressphoto agency b.v./Alamy Images; 26: US NAVY/Reuters/Landov; 27: Stocktrek Images/Getty Images; 28, 29 background: eranicle/Shutterstock, Inc.; 28 top: Time Life Pictures/Getty Images; 28 bottom: Leemage/Getty Images; 29 top: Niday Picture Library/Alamy Images; 29 bottom: The Granger Collection; 30: Photo 12/Getty Images; 32: Newagen Archive/The Image Works; 33: Rue des Archives/The Granger Collection; 34: ullstein bild/The Granger Collection; 35: AP Images; 36: Popperfoto/Getty Images; 37 left: UNEP/The Image Works; 37 right: Stephen Saks Photography/Alamy Images; 38: Mass Communication Specialist 2nd Class Daniel M. Young/U.S. Navy; 40: Mass Communication Specialist 1st Class Joshua J. Wahl/U.S. Navy; 41: Mass Communication Specialist Second Class Aidan P. Campbell/U.S. Navy; 42: Finnbarr Webster/Alamy Images; 43: Dirscherl Reinhard/age fotostock; 44: WINDN/AP Images.

J 623.82 MARSICO

Marsico, Katie.
Warships

                                    SEAST

R4002233447

SOUTHEAST
Atlanta-Fulton Public Library